Tropical Temporariness

Vatsala Radhakeesoon

(Haiku/Short Poems)

TRANSCENDENT ZERO PRESS
HOUSTON, TEXAS

Copyright © 2019, Vatsala Radhakeesoon

PUBLISHED BY TRANSCENDENT ZERO PRESS
www.transcendentzeropress.org

All rights reserved. No part or parts of this book may be reproduced in any format whether electronic or in print except as brief portions used in reviews, without the expressed written consent of Transcendent Zero Press, or of the author Vatsala Radhakeesoon.

ISBN-13: 978-1-946460-14-1
Library of Congress Control Number: 2019904858

Printed in the United States of America

Transcendent Zero Press
16429 El Camino Real Apt. #7
Houston, TX 77062

Cover art: "Morne au petit matin" (Morne as seen at dawn), painting by Pascal Lagesse

FIRST EDITION

Tropical Temporariness

Vatsala Radhakeesoon

(Haiku/Short Poems)

Other books by Vatsala Radhakeesoon

Unconditional Thread (Alien Buddha Press USA, 2019)

Journey to Victory and Freedom
Co-authored with author Sundeep Verma (Alien Buddha Press, USA, 2019)

Guitar of Love (Real Vision Inc Publishing, UK, 2018)

Smile Little Butterfly (Alien Buddha Press, USA, 2018)

L'aurore de la Sagesse (French Poetry) (Scarlet Leaf Publishing House, Canada, 2018)

Hope (President's Funds for Creative Writing, Mauritius, 2018)

Depth of the River (Scarlet Leaf Publishing House, Canada, 2017)

When Solitude Speaks (Ministry of Arts and Culture, Mauritius, 2013)

Dedication

I dedicate this book to all Mauritians, poetry-lovers, travelers and historians

Acknowledgements

I'm grateful to God for sustaining my inspiration and giving me the strength to write daily.

I also thank my sister, Sharda and my brothers, Umesh and Comal for their continual support while I've been writing this book.

Author's Note

In December 2018, due to some accumulated stress in my professional and personal life my health shouted "Halt!" Doctors advised me to slow down. Close family members believed I have over-worked. That was quite true. After having written 7 poetry books in solo and co-authored 1 philosophical book, I felt a burnout for the first time in my life. As a result of this, I decided to stay much deeply connected to God, nature, pets and music.

One sunny morning while watching the blue Mauritian sky, an inner voice within me said, "Rise! You can do it! Try something new, something lighter." After having written free verse and rhyming poetry, for more than 25 years, finally the idea of writing shorter poems emerged in my mind. Originating from Japanese poetry, haiku in English have always been my favorites as they instantly connect humankind to the power of Nature, create an aura of mystery at times and the last line of a well-written haiku often makes us reflect upon, question about and observe a particular natural environment. Thus, I decided to write "Tropical Temporariness", a collection of 42 haiku depicting the natural beauty of the landscapes and various touristic spots of my native exotic island, Mauritius. Some of the poems are supported by photos from professional photographers after they granted their permission to use them.

"Tropical" mainly refers to Mauritius being a tropical island in the Indian Ocean, southern hemisphere. "Temporariness" comes from the philosophical fact that everything is temporary. Even when we observe nature – the sunrise, sunset, appearance of a mountain at a particular time of the day or season are all momentary.

Tropical Temporariness may also be considered as my way to introduce my country to the world and invite all readers to discover this lovely gem of the Indian Ocean where the Dodo once lived.

Vatsala Radhakeesoon

April 2019

Preface

Brilliant Haiku About the Unique Island of Mauritius
Heath Brougher

Vatsala Radhakeesoon's *Tropical Temporariness* is a treasure trove filled with forty-two very powerfully informative and beautifully written haiku about her exotic homeland—the island of Mauritius. The island is a tropical paradise and due to its extremely unique and beyond gorgeous landscapes Mauritius was coined "Paradise Land" by Mark Twain. The term ended up sticking as many people still refer to it by this very title due to the island's unique and striking beauty and wildlife. Vatsala writes compelling and poignant haiku about many aspects of the beautiful island she calls home.

She writes brilliantly about the National Bird of Mauritius—the Dodo Bird. Such an amazing and unique creature as the Dodo Bird was driven to extinction when humans settled on the island. It's one of many fascinating topics that Vatsala makes sure to fit into the brilliant haiku that constitute this astounding collection. Her referencing of the Dodo Bird also brings up another important paradigm: although Dodo Birds have gone extinct, the exquisite eloquence and genius of Vatsala's writings must never suffer the same consequence. The fact that she has taken her brilliance to new heights by fitting so much genius into a mere forty-two haiku is more than enough proof that Vatsala Radhakeesoon is one of the most important and unique voices currently writing in the world of contemporary literature. This book is also very important in that it sheds an intense amount of light on an island that many people in the world don't know much about. It's quite amazing the amount of information Radhakeesoon is able to pack into these perfectly worded haiku which simultaneously sparkle with scintillating language yet still convey important information—a feat often attempted but rarely pulled off with such acumen of the English language.

Along with these eloquent haiku *Tropical Temporariness* is also filled with breathtaking pictures of the sheer beauty and wonder of the unique island of Mauritius. These pictures really help to top off an already brilliant book. It is almost as if this collection contains an overdose of information and imagery as the pictures help to fully propel this book into a new sphere of blended beauty and brilliance. The importance of this book, however, *cannot* be understated. The utter genius of Vatsala Radhakeesoon's writing is obvious but the pictures and the utter mystique of Mauritius are what really help to push this book over the edge and into the category of a "must-read." This is a book that could, honestly, be used to teach in schools due to the brilliant writing and the importance of the subject matter within, which, unfortunately, is not at the moment properly taught in public school curriculums. *Tropical Temporariness* is a book that could be used as a tool to fill that far-too-wide gap of knowledge about one of the most amazing places on the face of the Earth. Kudos to Vatsala Radhakeesoon, not just for her staggeringly brilliant haiku, but for helping to shed more light on Mauritius—one of the most fascinating places on the entire planet, "Paradise Land," where the Dodo Bird once roamed and where there is exotic beauty around every corner. Just like the astounding haiku and beautiful pictures that thrive in a state of full-blown brilliance in this book.

1.

Independent wind
blows through quadricolour flag
Belongingness breathes

2.

Summer summing heat
Island under *flamboyant**
singing some relief

*flamboyant: Tropical tree bearing red flowers

3.

Early morning rays
Tropical sky emits joy
Pigeons circle blue

4

Shelter of mountain
protecting the warm green town
Poetry muses

5

*Gris Gris** all complex
Dangerous sea calling death
Meet the true Teacher!

Gris Gris : Seaside situated in the southern part of Mauritius.
Gris Gris is considered to be mystic and dangerous.

6

A dot-like island
emerging from volcano
holds a mystic bird

7

The sun greys the mall
Technology meets nature
Vast sky expands stars

8

Pink evening clouds wink
Fluffy candy floss awaits
delicious soft rest

9

Leaves shake wrath
Clouds pour abundance of tears
Thunderstorm kills lies

10

Capital city
Cherishing harbour daily
Always eye catchy

11

The extinct *Dodo**
Subject arising debate
Souvenirs now smile

*Dodo: The national bird of Mauritius. Dodoes live on the island during the Dutch rule of Mauritius.

12

The tropical sun
A natural soft suntan
Equality- land

13

Mauritian winter
Without snow but gloomy breeze
Tea is in the air

14

The tropical cat
Short furred and energetic
glitters in the sun

15

Voices of sailors
In seashells of history
Echo in sea waves

16

The summer night breeze
Cooling effect on the ground
Island rejoices

17

Stars blink in the sky
Silence stirs the subconscious
Nature becomes wise

18

Soft sandy beaches
An antidote for grey stress
Nature hums wisdom

19

Serene *Grand Bassin**
Pilgrimage motivates souls
Cosmic dance is pleased

Grand Bassin: A lake considered to be sacred. Mauritian Hindus go there to perform religious ceremonies on the occasion of Maha Shivaratree festival.

20

Span of fifty years
Greenery suddenly grins
*Talipot** is back

* *Talipot*: A tropical tree found in the botanical garden of Mauritius. It bears flowers only every 50-100 years.

21

Slavery is dead
The *ravann** resonates joy
The sea swirls Sega

* *ravann*: A circular musical instrument used in the traditional songs and dances of Mauritius, the Sega.

22

Greenery unchained
Cruel masters have no say
Sugar is sweeter

23

Technology pours
Amidst the tropical trees
Here stands green city

24

The crescent moon smiles
Cool rays caress pensive rays
A kiss in the sea

25

Heated weary ground
Fully soaked in summer rain
plants re-energize

26

Anxious cute bats mourn
Wildlife claims its wise birthrights
Shelter my island!

27

Early morning time
A fish is caught in the net
Sea of painful tears

28

Wise *Corps de Garde**
Strong armour of hectic towns
The hearts of clouds melt

* *Corps de Garde* : Mountain sheltering Rose-Hill
and Quatre-Bornes towns in Mauritius.

29

Rainbow in vast sky
Rainbow resting on ground too
*Seven Coloured Earth**

* *Seven Coloured Earth*: Earth dunes of seven colours located
in the western part of the island.

30

Cyclonic fury
Heavy rainfall churning *dot**
Patience waltzing hearts

*dot: Mauritius appears as a dot on a world map. Thus, the dot refers to Mauritius.

31

Summer and winter
Only two seasons sailing
Hello Mauritius!

32

Animals tamed
Adorable *Casela**
Dream of escaping

Casela: A nature park of Mauritius that consists of birds and animal parks, safari, discovery centre and mountain kingdoms.

33

Hot *February**
Witnesses forceful cyclones
Calmness whispers "Swim!"

February: It is summer in Mauritius from November to April. February is the hottest month.

34

Orange blissful sky
Opening eyes of *Palmar**
Divine reflections

* *Palmar*: refers to Palmar beach found in the eastern region of Mauritius.

35

August, coldest month
The sun spreads warm rays blanket
Grey cold nostalgia

36

Eye of history
At *Chateau Labourdonnais**
*Cuisine Creole** grins

**Chateau Labourdonnais*: Mahe de Labourdonnais was the French Governor during French rule of Mauritius. Chateau Labourdonnais was his residence in the northern part of the island.

Cusine Creole: Food typically of Mauritian style including seafood

37

Blend fire red and blue
Primary colours unite
Vast *flamboyant* tree

38

Lovely *pink pigeon**
Unique fauna of island
often meets in books

* *pink pigeon*: An endemic pigeon of Mauritius that was about to be extinct but some have been saved. This bird is rarely seen though.

39

Starfish on the beach
Between water and dry sand
Waves calling again

40

Gracefulness in blue
Technology rushes by
Soft *paille en queue** flies

* *paille en queue* : A tropical bird whose long tail is remarkable
even from a distance.
Paille en queue is also an aircraft of Air Mauritius.

41

Echoing around
Dodo has met extinction
Now save the *Kestrels* *

* *Kestrels*: Endangered bird of Mauritius. They have been saved but are rare.

42

Summer or winter
Blue lagoon on travel map
The *Paradise Land**

* *Paradise Land* : Mauritius is often called the Paradise Land
for its blue sky, sea, sand, sun , flora and fauna.
Mark Twain first called it the Paradise Land when he visited the island.

Author Bio

Born in the exotic island Mauritius in 1977, Vatsala Radhakeesoon is the author of eight poetry books and one co-authored philosophical book. She started writing poems in English at the age of 14 and kept expanding her poetic skills in other languages such as French, Mauritian Kreol and Hindi. Vatsala Radhakeesoon is one of the representatives of Immagine and Poesia, an Italy based literary movement uniting artists and poets' works. She has been selected as one of the poets for Guido Gozzano Poetry contest, 2016, 2017, and 2018. Vatsala currently lives at Rose-Hill, Mauritius and is a literary translator, interviewer and reviewer.

Tropical Temporariness (Photo credits)

Haiku 1 : Mauritian Flag – Image by Ronny K , Pixabay

Haiku 2: Flamboyant tree – Image by MojcaJJ, Pixabay

Haiku 4: Mountain Sheltering- Photo by Gerard Peka

Haiku 5: Gris Gris sea - Photo by Gerard Peka

Haiku 10 : Port-Louis- Image by Irshad Rahimbux, Pixabay

Haiku 11: The Dodo (black and white pic)- Image by OpenClipart- vectors, Pixabay

Haiku 12: Mauritian Sun/Sunny Day- Image by Mueslimuse, Pixabay

Haiku 15: Sea waves- Photo by Ravi Bhaugmonea

Haiku 18: Soft sandy beaches- Photo by Ravi Bhaugmonea

Haiku 19:
Grand Bassin 1- Photo by Ravi Bhaugmonea
Grand Bassin 2 – Photo by Ravi Bhaugmonea

Haiku 26 : Bats of Mauritius- Photo by Keshav Nauthoo

Haiku 28: Corps de Garde mountain - Photo by Gerard Peka

Haiku 29 : Seven Colored Earth – Image by Nici Keil, Pixabay

Haiku 37 : Flamboyant Tree – Photo by Gerard Peka

Haiku 38 :
Pink Pigeon 1- Photo by Keshav Nauthoo
Pink pigeon 2- Photo by Keshav Nauthoo

Haiku 40: Paille en queue- Photo by Keshav Nauthoo

Haiku 42- Paradise Land –Photo by Ravi Bhaugmonea

www.ingramcontent.com/pod-product-compliance
Lightning Source LLC
Chambersburg PA
CBHW041808040426
42449CB00001B/18